Moving Beyond Abuse

Stories and Questions for Women Who Have Lived with Abuse

By Kay-Laurel Fischer and Michael F. McGrane

FIELDSTONE
ALLIANCE

SAINT PAUL
MINNESOTA

Manufactured in the United States of America
Fourth printing, November 2004

ISBN 0-940069-15-6

Edited by Jeanne Engelmann and Vincent Hyman
Designed by Rebecca Andrews

About the Publisher
The Amherst H. Wilder Foundation is one of the
largest and oldest endowed human service and
community development organizations in the
United States. Since 1906, the Wilder Foundation
has been providing health and human services that
help children and families grow strong, the elderly
age with dignity, and the community grow in its
ability to meet its own needs.

Amherst H. Wilder Foundation
Publishing Center
919 Lafond Avenue
Saint Paul, MN 55104

1-800-274-6024
www.wilder.org/pubs

Acknowledgments

A special thank you to Sheila Craig and Carol Evans for their contributions to this journal.

Contents

Introduction

Using the Guided Journal

Moving Beyond Abuse is a separate book that accompanies the sessions in the domestic abuse facilitator's guide, *Journey Beyond Abuse*. We hope you will use the journal to write your personal thoughts on topics related to abuse in general as well as those related to your own personal experiences.

The journal is intended to:

- Reinforce what you learn in the women's domestic abuse group.
- Help you further explore your thoughts on any individual topic related to abuse.
- Encourage future journaling as a way to address personal issues, ideas, thoughts, and feelings.

Topics in this journal correspond to topics explored in the group. For each topic, you'll find both a story and a series of questions. The stories and questions in this journal relate to key ideas taught within the group. Each story is based on real situations experienced by women who have had a variety of experiences and possess varying degrees of insight into their situations. Our hope is that these stories will help you understand that you are not alone in your experiences of abuse. The activities in this journal are designed to help you connect the general ideas discussed in group with your specific experiences. It is this connection that helps healing begin.

When you use this journal, you must consider whether or not safety is an issue. You must decide if it is safe for you to have a journal in your possession. You will need to find a safe place to keep it so that your life and private thoughts will not be violated. You must consider what is best for your particular situation.

If you decide you cannot feel safe with the journal in your possession, consider keeping it elsewhere—out of the house, perhaps with a friend. Although this involves going to a different location to write in the journal, it may be the best plan. It may be wise to err on the side of safety.

Eight Program Principles

1. Abuse is a learned behavior that has negative consequences for women and children.
2. Abuse is reinforced by our society.
3. Abuse can be passed on from generation to generation.
4. There is no justification for abuse.
5. Women are not responsible for a partner's abusive behavior nor can they control a partner's abusive behavior.
6. Chemical abuse and violence are two separate issues that need to be addressed separately.
7. Issues of abuse need to be initially addressed in a setting that is separate from the abusive person.
8. Each woman has her own answers and timing for addressing her issues related to abuse.

Program Goals

1. To define and recognize abusive behaviors.
2. To understand how abuse is impacting women's and children's lives.
3. To get support and encouragement from other women.
4. To learn to identify and express feelings.
5. To break down isolation.
6. To stop minimization of the abuse.
7. To understand that women are not to blame for a partner's abusive behavior.
8. To focus on the healing of self.
9. To provide information about available resources.
10. To support the empowerment process for women.

Stories and Questions

"I Almost Didn't Go"

I just got home from my first women's domestic abuse group. What a surprise! I can hardly believe how good I feel. The women I met tonight were so nice and understanding. And to think, I almost didn't go. I was so scared and nervous I could hardly get out of the car and walk into the building.

When the group started, everyone else looked pretty nervous too. Then the group leader told us she is always nervous on the first night of group. Hm! We played this game called the "Big Wind Blows." It seemed kind of stupid at first when it was explained, but we all had a pretty good time playing it, and everyone seemed to relax.

After the break, the group leader said we were going to start talking about our experiences related to abuse. I didn't volunteer to talk tonight, but two other women did. One woman told about how mad her husband got at her right before she was leaving for the group. He asked her if she was going to her "male bashing party." Wow, could I relate. Stan tried really hard to keep me from going to this group tonight, too, by getting home late and making sure the gas tank was empty. He can't stop me though because Jill says I can use her car anytime.

Another woman, Mary, started to cry when she told about how scared she is of her ex-husband. He won't leave her alone and shows up wherever she is going. She said she was so embarrassed and feels so stupid. Every group member assured Mary she wasn't stupid for what was happening and that she wasn't doing anything to cause him to follow her. We also told her that we hoped she wouldn't feel embarrassed any longer for his scary behavior. Mary looked like she felt better after we all gave our support.

This first session at group was way beyond what I ever expected it to be and I feel so much better knowing I'm not the only person with these problems. I can hardly wait until next week's group. I'm excited about this group and hope it can help me.

Introduction to Group

1. How did you feel at the start of the first group session?

   At first I felt _____

   because _____

   _____

   _____

   _____

   _____

2. How did you feel at the close of the group session?

   At the end of the group I felt _____

   because _____

   _____

   _____

   _____

   _____

3. How do you feel about returning to the next session?

   _____

   _____

   _____

   _____

4. What are the most important things you learned during this session?

   I learned _____

   _____

   _____

   _____

   I learned _____

   _____

   _____

   _____

   I learned _____

   _____

   _____

   _____

5. Do you especially agree with some points in the Eight Program Principles?

   I agreed with: _____

   _____

   _____

   _____

   _____

6. Did you disagree with some of the Eight Program Principles? __ yes __ no
   If yes, which did you disagree with and why?

   I disagreed with principle # ____ *because* _____

   _____

   _____

   _____

   _____

7. Did any one principle shock or surprise you? __ yes __ no
   If yes, which one and why?

   _____

   _____

   _____

   _____

8. Which of the program goals would you especially like to address?

   I would like to work on _____ *because* _____

   _____

   _____

   _____

   _____

   I would also like to work on _____ *because* _____

   _____

   _____

   _____

   _____

9. Do you feel safe in this group?

___ *yes, because* _____

_____

_____

_____

___ *no, because* _____

_____

_____

_____

10. Do you have any fears or concerns about the group? ___ yes ___ no

If yes, what concerns you and why?

_____

_____

_____

_____

11. Did you make a connection with anyone in the group? ___ yes ___ no

If yes, with whom? _____

What did you like about her? _____

_____

_____

_____

_____

"What An Eye Opener"

I had mixed feelings about attending a domestic abuse women's group but I knew I needed to try to figure out what was happening in my life. I was so uncertain if this was the right thing for me to be doing. I felt like I was betraying Bill because I still believe he's really not a bad guy and doesn't mean to hurt me and the kids.

Except for the two times that Bill slapped me and threw me up against the wall, he has never really hurt me and it was really my fault that he got so mad those times. I thought if I hadn't called the police after the first time he hurt me, maybe he wouldn't have slapped me around the second time.

It's hard to think of what Bill does as abuse. But then Shawma was telling about some really similar things her boyfriend did to her and how she left him because of his abuse. That's what she called it — abuse. Even though I didn't say anything about Bill in group, I was thinking about the things he's done to me and how much they were like what happened to Shawma.

When the group had "Defining Abuse" as a topic, I was surprised to learn what abuse really is. We defined abuse in the four primary areas of physical, verbal, sexual, and emotional. I began to see how many of the definitions felt familiar to me. For example, I had never thought of Bill's affair as being abusive. And then there was all the lying that he did when he was involved with Jane from his office. I had thought maybe I was going crazy and had only imagined that I smelled perfume on his clothes. He began accusing *me* of having an affair and making me feel guilty about questioning him. Here all along it wasn't me that did anything wrong. It was one big lie. His lie.

I could go on and on about the things that were defined as abusive that I had never thought of as abuse before. What an eye opener! The group leader said that the feelings of violation are much the same for women no matter how the abuse occurs. The leader also talked about how it feels to "name" what is happening in our lives and how that brings on a new reality for many of us. I guess this group is where I belong after all.

Defining Abuse

1. List several examples of each type of abuse you have experienced.

PHYSICAL	VERBAL

SEXUAL	EMOTIONAL

2. Now that you've had a chance to identify different types of abuse that you have experienced, do you still think you "caused" it to happen? Record your feelings about your role in the abusive experiences you mentioned on the previous page.

_____

_____

_____

_____

_____

_____

_____

_____

3. In the future, how will you know when you're being abused? List what you think are the key signs of abuse below.

I know when a situation has become abusive to me when:

a. _____

_____

b. _____

_____

c. _____

_____

4. When you experience abuse in the future, who can you talk with about it?

I will talk with:

a. _____

b. _____

c. _____

5. What can you do to care for yourself? List several things, large or small, that you can do to nurture your self-esteem (don't forget to mention things you just plain enjoy or have fun doing).

a. _____

b. _____

c. _____

d. _____

e. _____

6. Draw your own "House of Abuse" (a large house divided into nine rooms).

a. Write physical, emotional, sexual, and verbal abuse in each of four rooms and write in some examples of each type of abuse you have experienced from activity #1 listed above.

b. Now think of other types of abuse you have experienced and write these in the remaining five rooms (for example, child abuse, isolation, intimidation, alcohol and drugs, male privilege).

c. How does it feel to see the abuse you have experienced illustrated in this way?

   I feel _____

   _____

d. If the perpetrator "cleans out" one room of the house (such as stopping his physical abuse) without cleaning out the others, is he still abusive?

   Please explain_____

   _____

   _____

"The Escalation, Explosion, and Honeymoon"

A lot of things started to make sense tonight in group when our group leader explained what she called the "Pattern of Abuse." I felt like I wasn't the crazy one anymore. First she explained the three stages of abuse—escalation, explosion, and honeymoon—and then we drew our own pattern of abuse. As I began to think about my relationship with Ron, I began to draw a roller coaster. Later we shared our drawings. When it was my turn, I said that my pattern of abuse begins with arguments between Ron and me when I find out about lies he has told me. The arguments escalate, the roller coaster begins the ascent up the hill with both of us yelling at each other. At the explosion stage, we are at the top of the coaster, Ron pushes and threatens me, I begin to cry, he swears at me, then he leaves. The roller coaster rolls down the tracks into the honeymoon stage when Ron returns with apologies and flowers. He even looks like he's really sorry and promises it won't happen again. I always wonder, "How long will the peace last this time?" The tension builds again as I worry about if I will say something that might set him off yet another time.

Several women in my group said that they had also felt that they had been on a roller coaster ride in their relationships. We talked about how so many of us feel hope for a change during the honeymoon phase that we tend to forget about the explosion part of the cycle.

I drove home thinking I want to remember all parts of the abuse pattern. I decided I'm going to begin journaling my thoughts and feelings after roller coaster situations with Ron. I think this will help me think more clearly and not feel so responsible for his abuse.

Patterns of Abuse

1. Describe a typical example in your life of each of the three stages of escalation:

   Example of escalation: _____

   _____

   _____

   Example of explosion/abuse: _____

   _____

   _____

   Example of aftermath/honeymoon: _____

   _____

   _____

2. How do you now view the aftermath or honeymoon behavior pattern in your relationship? Do you trust the behavior and promises?

   I see the aftermath behavior as: _____

   _____

   _____

   _____

3. How can you best respond to the aftermath behavior?

   I can:

   a. _____

   _____

   b. _____

   _____

   c. _____

   _____

4. Summarize what you have learned about the cycle of violence as it applies to your life.

   _____

   _____

   _____

   _____

   _____

   _____

"We Are So Used to Being Caretakers"

I hadn't planned on talking in group tonight. I'm not used to sharing my feelings but when I heard tonight's topic, "What Keeps Women in Abusive Relationships," I suddenly found myself speaking out about how unhappy and confused I feel in my marriage. The last 8 of my 12 married years have felt pretty miserable. My husband has been so verbally abusive to me that most of the time I feel incapable of doing anything right.

I've felt more and more unhappy and recently have had serious thoughts and plans to move out of the house. However, when I told my three children about my plans to move out, they became *so* upset—they cried and begged me not to break up the family. Now I feel even more confused and like I'm the bad guy in this situation. Why do I feel so guilty if I haven't done anything wrong? I feel like I will be blamed for the breakup, but isn't it his abuse that caused it?

After I was done sharing my feelings in group, two other women said they had similar feelings and experiences. Yvette said it's hard not to feel responsible for our families when we are so used to being the caretakers. Yvette said that when she separated from her partner, it took her children about a year to adjust to the change, but now she and the children are happier than they've ever been. Several other women agreed that this is not an easy decision for any woman to make and a decision that no one can make for me.

On the way home I thought about everything that was said and all the feedback I heard tonight in group. It felt so good to share my unhappy feelings and finally have some people who care and understand. It was also nice to hear that I don't have to make a decision today or tomorrow. I think I still have some things to sort out before I decide what to do next.

What Keeps Women in Abusive Relationships?

1. Was it helpful for you to hear other women describe and acknowledge the reasons that keep (or kept) them in their abusive relationships? Explain.

_____

_____

_____

_____

_____

_____

_____

_____

_____

_____

_____

_____

_____

_____

_____

_____

2. List the five most important reasons that keep you in an abusive relationship.

a. _____

b. _____

c. _____

d. _____

e. _____

3. How have you addressed these reasons to reduce some of the power they may have over you?

a. _____

b. _____

c. _____

d. _____

e. _____

4. Many people believe that our society condones and allows abuse. Do you agree? If so, how does this *personally* impact you? How has it contributed to your staying in an abusive relationship?

_____

_____

_____

_____

_____

_____

_____

_____

_____

_____

_____

_____

_____

_____

5. List some reasons that you believe answer the question, "Why do men abuse/batter women?"

_____

_____

_____

_____

_____

_____

_____

_____

_____

_____

_____

_____

_____

_____

6. Is there any justification for these reasons? Explain your answer.

_____

_____

_____

_____

_____

_____

_____

_____

_____

_____

_____

_____

_____

_____

7. Women often feel ashamed of staying in an abusive relationship. Can you think of ways to address any shame you might be experiencing?

_____

_____

_____

_____

_____

_____

_____

_____

_____

_____

_____

_____

_____

_____

"I Call It Mind Games"

I still remember the night I realized I wasn't crazy. It was the third session of my women's abuse group and the counselor was writing examples of emotional abuse on the chalkboard...lying, intimidation...saying one thing while doing another. It seemed she was talking about my life—all the things that made me think something was wrong with me. It had been going on for so long that I thought I was the one who was crazy. And Jim had been telling me just that for years. Every time he got upset he called me "Psycho Bitch" and said that I didn't deserve to live.

He always told me that it was my fault that we didn't have any friends...that I wasn't smart enough to carry on a decent conversation with anyone. Yet, every time I started to talk, he interrupted me. And he couldn't stand my friends. He said they were boring and he insulted them or sat in the living room reading when they came over. They just quit coming after awhile. And he didn't want me to go over to their houses because he said they were just trying to brainwash me against him because they didn't understand him. He did the same thing to my family.

Life around our house was like walking on pins and needles. The kids were afraid of him and went to their rooms as soon as Jim walked in the door. He never listened to them, or me for that matter, and he'd keep on reading or mumble something if one of us said anything to him. It was obvious he didn't care about what we were saying. Nothing we *ever* did was good enough for him. He criticized Joey because he stuttered and had developed a nervous tic that drove Jim crazy. He was always on Joey's case.

And Amanda barely said anything around him. She seemed to try to blend into the woodwork. Once she made his favorite pudding for dessert, spent all afternoon on it, and he didn't even notice. She cried a lot, too. In fact, we both cried a lot. Life was pretty depressing.

But that night in group I finally realized that this wasn't right. It was called emotional or psychological abuse. I call it head or mind games. He's got a million of them. And the kids and I aren't the problem. Jim needs to learn to control his behavior instead of taking all his frustration out on us. All we can do is take care of ourselves.

Emotional Abuse

1. How would you define emotional abuse?

_____

_____

_____

_____

_____

2. List specific ways that you feel emotionally abused by a partner.

   I feel emotionally abused when:

   a. _____

   b. _____

   c. _____

3. When these situations occur, how do you feel?

   When any of the situations I listed in #2 happen, I most often feel:

   _____

   _____

   _____

   _____

   _____

4. How does emotional abuse affect you?

   a. What scars of emotional abuse do you have? Describe. _____

   _____

   _____

   _____

   _____

   _____

   b. Are the effects long-lasting? Describe. _____

   _____

   _____

   _____

   _____

   _____

5. Did you experience emotional abuse in your childhood? ___ yes ___ no

   If yes, from whom? _____

   What happened? _____

   _____

   _____

   _____

   _____

   _____

6. How has emotional abuse affected you?

   Your self-esteem? _____

   _____

   Your relationships?_____

   _____

   Your development as a person? _____

   _____

   Your abilities/competency?_____

   _____

   Your ability to make decisions? _____

   _____

7. In what specific ways are you dependent on your partner to get your needs met?

   _____

   _____

   _____

   In what ways is your partner dependent on you to get his needs met?

   _____

   _____

   _____

   Do you need to make any changes on how you get your needs met?

   _____

   _____

   _____

8. Following are two psychological needs we all have:
   - A sense of being worthwhile.
   - A need for feeling and giving love.

   Is your partner helping or harming you with these basic needs?
   Please explain. _____

   _____

   _____

   _____

   _____

   _____

   _____

   _____

   _____

   _____

   _____

   _____

   _____

   _____

   _____

9. List some ways in which you can care for yourself when you feel
   emotionally abused:

   a. _____

   _____

   _____

   _____

   b. _____

   _____

   _____

   _____

   c. _____

   _____

   _____

   _____

"It Had Been Simmering Inside Me for Years"

It wasn't until I attended tonight's group that I could let myself feel the anger that I had been stuffing all those years with Alfonso. It wasn't safe to tell him. I would probably have been killed. But the anger was still there. I had just stuffed it inside and it had been simmering inside of me for years.

In group we did this exercise where we wrote a letter to someone telling them how angry we were with them. I was afraid to do it, even in group. I didn't want to touch all that anger because I was afraid of what might happen. But the counselor said we should try to put it down on paper just to let the anger out.

I found myself getting upset just trying to write the words. My heart was racing and my hands were shaking. But I did it. I wrote out all the anger and hurt and disappointment I had felt over many years.

It wasn't even the physical abuse that hurt the most. It was all the times he told me that I was stupid and worthless, all the times he said it in front of the kids and other people. That was what hurt the most. The words, the looks, the ignoring me. And what really makes me mad is that I believed it too. I had lived my life to please him and all I ever got was put-downs. He had been putting me down for so long and in so many ways that I had no doubt in my mind that he was right.

It wasn't until I started attending my group that I started feeling better about myself. All these other women think I'm okay. They like me and treat me with respect. I'm starting to think I might be okay myself. I'm starting to care about me.

When I finished writing the letter, I felt good. I read it out loud to the group and it felt like a big weight had been lifted. And the counselors and group were so kind and supportive. They understood. No one criticized me. I felt free. I knew I couldn't take the letter home. It wasn't safe. But I didn't want to destroy it either. So I put it in an envelope with my name on it and asked one of the counselors to keep it in a safe place for me. Maybe some day I will get it back from the counselor and show it to someone.

Anger about Abuse

1. As a child, what happened if you tried to express your anger?

_____

_____

_____

_____

_____

_____

_____

_____

2. What messages did that teach you about expressing anger?

I learned: _____

_____

_____

_____

_____

_____

_____

_____

3. Have you felt depressed when you were angry? ___ yes ___ no

If yes, describe that combination of feelings: _____

_____

_____

_____

_____

_____

_____

_____

4. Does your anger ever feel positive? Please describe:

_____

_____

_____

_____

_____

_____

_____

_____

_____

Does your anger feel negative? Describe: _____

_____

_____

_____

_____

_____

_____

_____

_____

5. What are some signs that tell you you're feeling angry?

_____

_____

_____

_____

_____

_____

_____

_____

6. How do you express your anger?

_____

_____

_____

_____

_____

_____

_____

7. Is it safe for you to express your anger to others?

_____

_____

_____

_____

_____

_____

_____

8. Is it safe for you to ignore your anger?

_____

_____

_____

_____

_____

_____

_____

9. Are you currently angry with someone?

Who? _____

Is there any constructive thing you can do about it? _____

_____

_____

_____

_____

_____

_____

"I'm Not Sure I Can Ever Forgive Him for That Night"

Here is the most hurtful thing I remember:

My mom has just died, my sister is probably paralyzed from a fall, and I am eight months pregnant and feeling terribly trapped in a hotel room with my husband. Of course, Daryl is acting loving and concerned about my health and says he doesn't want me to suffer any undu stress, but I don't trust him. He has talked me into leaving my family behind at the mortuary and not visiting my sister in the hospital. All of this, of course, is in the name of protecting me and our soon to be born first child. We have just traveled a long distance to be with my family and now he is keeping me from them. We just got settled into bed and Daryl decides he wants to have sex. He will not take "no" for an answer and forces me to do what I don't enjoy doing. I'm not sure I can ever forgive him for that night so very many years ago when he was really only thinking of himself and not my pain at all.

The group was really angry at Daryl when I told my story. One group member gasped and wondered how dare he take me away from the family I had just traveled so far to be with on this tragic day. And then, to add to everything else, the group was once again having to discuss whether or not men have the right to have sex whenever they want it. I'm sick of analyzing that and want to tell Daryl he can never touch me again as long as he lives without my permission. Pregnant or not, the group thought that he didn't have the right to dictate when I could be at the mortuary and the hospital. That never even occurred to me at the time. The group found it interesting that he wanted to protect me from the stress related to my family's tragedies but wasn't too concerned about my body undergoing stress from unwanted sexual activity. The group was so kind and loving to me as I told my "most hurtful incident" and once again grieved the loss of my mother and the condition of my sister. They said over and over how very selfish and controlling Daryl was that night and that I had a right to still have these angry and hurt feelings. They hoped that I could let go of the hurt for my own sake in the near future.

Most Hurtful Incident

1. How did you feel when you listened to the abuse story of another group member?

___ *I felt sorry for her.*   ___ *I felt angry with her for putting up with it.*

___ *I felt sad.*   ___ *I felt uncomfortable while listening.*

I also felt _____

_____

_____

_____

2. Do you know why you felt the way you did? Please explain.

I felt _____

because _____

_____

_____

_____

3. Name the elements in her story that compared to your own.

These things also happened to me:

a. _____

b. _____

c. _____

d. _____

4. Was there anything you would like to have said to her that you weren't able to say in group? ___ yes ___ no

If yes, what do you wish you could have said?

_____

_____

_____

_____

_____

_____

_____

_____

"No Way Are You Stupid!"

Tonight we talked about negative messages in group and how they have affected us. I was surprised at how I felt when I recognized some of the things mother had been saying to me for years and how those messages made me feel about myself.

It was really hard to write them down on paper. These were the things I didn't like to hear about myself and it hurt to write them. But something felt good about doing it. We talked in group about how these messages had become a part of how we see ourselves. And the real shock was to realize that they weren't necessarily true or accurate.

When I read one of my negative messages out loud the group said, "No way are you stupid." They gave me all kinds of examples of ways they thought I was quite the opposite. They thought I was smart! The leader suggested that every time the feeling that I was stupid came up, I should say to myself, "I am an intelligent woman." I have tried it and it really feels good!

Impact of Negative Messages

1. List some of the negative messages you heard as a child from one of your parents. In each case, mention how you felt and how you reacted:

I was told: *I felt:*   *I reacted by:*

a. _____

_____

_____

_____

b. _____

_____

_____

_____

c. _____

_____

_____

_____

2. List some names you have been called and describe your feelings:

I have been called: *By:*   *When I am called this, I feel like:*

a. _____

_____

_____

_____

b. _____

_____

_____

_____

c. _____

_____

_____

_____

3. Write one negative message that has had significant impact on you:

_____

_____

_____

_____

_____

_____

I can rewrite this message into a positive message as follows:

_____

_____

_____

_____

_____

_____

_____

4. How have negative messages affected your self-esteem?

_____

_____

_____

_____

_____

_____

_____

_____

_____

_____

_____

_____

_____

_____

_____

_____

5. *I can refuse to accept the negative messages that others direct toward me by:*

a. _____

_____

_____

_____

_____

b. _____

_____

_____

_____

_____

c. _____

_____

_____

_____

_____

"We Must All Be Married to the Same Guy"

Until I went to my women's group, I had no idea that women who are being abused have so much in common. I was really surprised to hear other women tell what could be my story. When Sarah talked about how she doesn't answer the phone or the door sometimes for days, that could be me. The group leader said that isolation is common for women being abused. Then Carol started talking about her anger towards her husband, and I really related to that. When I got a chance, I told the group about all my anger at Phil.

Sometimes I feel so confused about what is going on at home and every person in the group agreed that they, too, often feel confused. All of us think that the abuse seems wrong but our husbands and boyfriends say we deserve it because of the way we act. Most of us said we feel ashamed of the abuse and don't like friends and neighbors knowing what's going on. I would leave but I'm so scared of being lonely. I wonder why I feel that way—Phil never talks to me anyway except when he's mad at me.

Wanda said in group one night, "We must all be married to the same guy." This really cracked the group up and pointed out how much we have in common.

It's been so good for me to hear all the experiences of the other women. It helps me to feel less crazy and to see that this abuse has not necessarily been my fault even though Phil said it is. I wish this group could go on forever. I'm really going to miss it when it's over. I can't remember feeling this good in a long time.

Common Experiences of Battered Women

Trauma	Isolation	Fear/Terror	Shame
Depression	Minimization	Anger/Rage	Grief and Loss
Fear of Loneliness	Post-Traumatic Stress	Confusion	Sadness

1. Choose one issue from the list above that you feel is important to explore. Explain why this issue in particular is key for you.

   I would like to further explore: _____

   because: _____

   _____

2. Are you feeling isolated right now? How does that feel?

   _____

   _____

3. What can you do to reduce isolation?

   a. _____

   b. _____

4. Does your partner try to control your activity? ___ yes ___no

   If yes, in what ways?_____

   _____

   What would you like to tell your partner about how his controlling your activity makes you feel: _____

   _____

   _____

   Is it safe to tell him these things? _____

5. What other common experiences would you like to address?

   _____

   _____

   _____

6. What can you do to address each of these experiences?

   _____

   _____

   _____

"It's Time to Break the Pattern"

I know what it's like to watch your father physically attack your mother. Tonight in group we discussed the impact of domestic abuse on children. I shared my story with the group. I grew up watching my mother being abused. I remember how scared I felt when they began to argue because I knew what would happen next. So I told myself I would never marry someone who was abusive.

I've been married to Sam for 15 years. We have a 14-year-old daughter, Sabrina. For the past 12 years of our marriage Sam has been verbally and physically abusive. I've watched Sabrina attempt to stop her father when he becomes physically abusive toward me. Sabrina will put herself in between Sam and me because she knows he won't hurt her. Sabrina and I haven't talked about these "bad times." Six months ago I decided to move out and Sabrina seems a lot happier, yet I still wonder what impact the violence has had on her.

I was surprised at how many other women in the group have had the same experience and worry about their children too. A couple of women encouraged me to begin talking with Sabrina about the abuse and trying to find out how she feels about it. Mary made a good point, saying that my mother never talked with me and I repeated the same pattern. It's time to break the pattern with Sabrina. I know it may take some time for Sabrina to open up—I just hope it's not too late.

Impact of Abuse on Children

1. As a child, did you witness an abusive situation between your parents or other significant adults in your life? ___ yes ___ no

   If yes, please describe the incident: _____

   _____

   _____

   _____

   _____

   _____

   _____

   _____

2. How did you feel as a child witnessing the event?

   _____

   _____

   _____

   _____

   _____

   _____

3. Which of these feelings do you think your children experience?

   _____

   _____

   _____

   _____

   _____

   _____

4. How do you think your children are responding to the abuse in your home?

   _____

   _____

   _____

   _____

   _____

   _____

5. Are your children exhibiting any emotional or behavioral problems that may be related to the abuse? Describe.

_____

_____

_____

_____

_____

_____

_____

_____

6. Do your children sometimes blame you for the abuse you experience? Take sides with the abuser? Think you could prevent the abuse? If yes, how do you handle this?

_____

_____

_____

_____

_____

_____

_____

_____

7. Children are playful, noisy, and creative. How has the abuse in the house affected this aspect of your children's lives?

_____

_____

_____

_____

_____

_____

_____

_____

8. Describe what you can tell your children to help them understand each of these ideas:

Children don't cause abuse.

To explain this, I would tell my kids: _____

_____

_____

_____

_____

_____

_____

_____

Expressing feelings is a good thing for kids to do.

To explain this, I would tell my kids: _____

_____

_____

_____

_____

_____

_____

_____

Kids can take specific steps to resolve conflict in their lives.

To explain this, I would tell my kids: _____

_____

_____

_____

_____

_____

_____

_____

"It Felt Good to Get Away"

My husband is a screamer and a yeller. He scares the kids with all his yelling but I just try to ignore him and wait until he's over whatever he's so mad about. I told my group about how he wakes me up in the middle of the night to yell at me. Sometimes this goes on for several hours. He demands that I answer him and his ridiculous accusations. I have all I can do not to start laughing at him. Since I have to be at work at 8:00 a.m. and need to be bright and alert on my job, this gets to be a problem when I'm so tired from him keeping me awake.

My group had a difficult time understanding why I'm not furious at Dan for disturbing my sleep. I guess I'm just so used to his childish behavior that I just don't think much about it. But the group did get me to agree that I should not be going to work so tired and frustrated from lack of sleep. We discussed assertiveness in group at length and it was suggested that I leave the bedroom and go sleep on the couch when Dan begins one of his tirades. Then I said that if that doesn't work, I would leave the house and go sleep at my sister's down the block. The group reminded me that I need to be sure my decision to assert myself felt safe and that I wouldn't get hurt if I did this.

Well, two nights ago Dan woke me because he was mad about money I had spent. I left to sleep on the couch. He kept yelling. I put my jacket and boots on over my pajamas and walked to my sister's at 2:00 a.m. I had warned her that this might happen and she let me in. I knew the kids would be fine and I would go home first thing in the morning.

I can't believe how good it felt to get away from Dan's middle-of-the-night yelling. It had never occurred to me before that I had a right to remove myself from his abuse. I think Dan is still wondering what happened to make me leave. I wonder if he'll ever realize how silly he sounds when he's yelling and that I usually don't pay attention to what he's saying anyway. We'll see! For now, I like this new plan to stop the yelling and feel good about asserting myself to be able to get more sleep.

Assertiveness

Read the following descriptions:

Passive: few opinions; needs are unimportant; avoids conflict; is often taken advantage of.

Aggressive: creates conflict; intimidating; demanding; hostile; attacking.

Passive-aggressive: resents others; mean-spirited; hurts through silence; intentionally forgetful.

Assertive: solves problems; uses "I" statements; communicates clearly; looks for win/win situations.

———•———

1. Which of these behaviors did you learn as a child? _____

   _____
   _____
   _____
   _____

   From whom?_____

   _____
   _____
   _____

2. Describe what you would be like as an assertive person. Name some situations, ways of communicating, or problem solving you would do differently.

   _____
   _____
   _____
   _____
   _____
   _____
   _____
   _____
   _____
   _____
   _____
   _____

3. How do you think others in your life (partner, children, extended family) would act if you behaved assertively? _____

_____

_____

_____

_____

_____

_____

4. Would it be safe for you to act assertively with your abusive partner? Describe what you think might happen. _____

_____

_____

_____

_____

_____

_____

5. Assertiveness means stating how you feel and what you want. Practice being assertive by filling in the following statements:

When I feel _____

_____

because of _____

_____

I need to _____

_____

and I want _____

_____

6. Name an assertive woman you respect _____

What specifically do you admire about this woman?

_____

_____

_____

_____

_____

_____

7. If you become assertive like this woman, what will you gain?

_____

_____

_____

_____

_____

_____

8. Are there any negative consequences you may experience by being assertive?

_____

_____

_____

_____

_____

_____

9. How might becoming assertive improve your boundaries with other people?

_____

_____

_____

_____

_____

"Joe Went into My Purse without Asking"

I am a 37-year-old with three children and an abusive husband. I have a good job with the county and lots of good friends at my work. I love going to work because I feel so good about my job and how my coworkers treat me.

One of my friends at work invited me to her daughter's wedding. I was so pleased to be invited and told my friend I would get back to her as soon as I knew if I could come or not. I put the invitation in my purse and promptly forgot about it.

When I went home that night, Joe went into my purse as he often does without asking. He found the invitation and immediately began to accuse me of everything from trying to hide from him what I was doing to cheating on him. We started to argue and, once again, I felt terrible because the kids had to suffer listening to us fight and being scared for me.

The group got mad when I told them how Joe goes into my purse all the time and then picks a fight over something he finds. I guess I've never thought much about how often he does that. The group told me that it is okay for me to get invited somewhere without Joe and that he has no right to start accusing me of anything and everything because of that. I think that part of the trap for me is that I start to feel like the whole thing is my fault because the kids so dislike it when there is chaos between Joe and me. Then I start to think that if only I hadn't accepted the invitation, Joe wouldn't have had a reason to be mad and the whole thing could have been avoided. The group and the group leader tried to help me see the flaws in my thinking. They pointed out that only Joe can be responsible for his behavior and that it is unfortunate that the kids get upset, but if it hadn't been the invitation, it probably would have been something else. I guess they're right, but it's really hard to see my kids look so scared.

The group says that Joe has bad boundaries and that he shouldn't go into my purse without my permission. I'm beginning to think they may have a point.

Boundaries

1. What is a boundary?

   A boundary is _____

   _____

   _____

2. When growing up, did your family have and respect boundaries?
   ___ yes ___ no

   Describe the boundaries respected (or violated) within your family of
   origin: _____

   _____

   _____

   _____

   _____

3. How did this early experience with boundaries affect you?

   _____

   _____

   _____

   _____

   _____

4. List specific boundary violations you are currently experiencing by a
   partner, family members, or friends.

   Boundary violation: **By whom:**

   a. _____

   b. _____

   c. _____

   d. _____

   e. _____

5. Can you change how you handle these boundary violations? How?

   a. _____

   b. _____

   c. _____

   d. _____

   e. _____

6. How is the abuse you experience connected to poor boundaries in your relationship?

_____

_____

_____

_____

_____

_____

_____

_____

7. Rate yourself on the following statements:

Scale: 1 = Never   2 = Rarely   3 = Sometimes   4 = Often   5 = Always

Statement:	**Rating:**
a. *I have trouble saying "no" to people*	_____
b. *People use my things without asking.*	_____
c. *It's hard to find time for myself.*	_____
d. *I tend not to tell people how they've hurt me.*	_____
e. *Family members assume I should be available at any time.*	_____

Look at the statements you rated "often" or "always." Are these areas in which other people violate your boundaries? Who and how?

_____

_____

_____

_____

_____

_____

_____

_____

_____

_____

_____

8. How might you address those who overstep their boundaries with you? List three possible solutions:

a. _____

_____

b. _____

_____

c. _____

_____

9. Do you overstep your boundaries with others? When, with whom, and how?

_____

_____

_____

_____

_____

_____

_____

_____

_____

_____

_____

"Sex and Sexuality Are Not the Same Thing"

Sex and sexuality are topics I have never felt comfortable talking about. When I was growing up, my mom didn't seem interested in explaining the "facts of life" or that even sex and sexuality were not the same thing! When I began to date Tim in college, he made me feel so beautiful and sexy! He used to tell me how nice I looked and I felt so good about myself and about being a woman.

Tonight's group topic "women and sexuality" really had me thinking about how I feel about my sexuality. I shared with the group that for the past 3-4 years all I've heard from Tim are demeaning and cruel comments about myself as a woman. When Tim is angry, he seems to take it out on me by making hurtful comments such as "you are a worthless woman." At times when we are out to eat with friends, Tim will say "why are you eating that, you're already overweight." The put-downs and criticisms have made me feel ugly. I find myself less and less interested in sex with Tim and wanting to say no to a sexual relationship with him, yet fearful if I refuse him. I guess I've felt I can't say no. Tim has told me that it's a wife's "duty" to have sex when the husband wants to. He'll also say things like, "I got more sex when I was single" or accuse me of having sex with someone else since I won't have sex with him.

I was surprised at the feedback from the group members. Two other women said they also have felt pressure from their husbands for a sexual relationship when they didn't feel comfortable about it. Jenny pointed out that I seemed to allow my feelings about my sexuality to come from how my husband treats me or messages he gives me. The group leader pointed out that this is a common pattern in women. We talked about ways to feel good about our bodies as they are and that we should be able to say no to sex without feeling guilty or fearful. It wasn't an easy topic to talk about but I did feel relief that other women had had similar experiences. I was glad to have a safe place to talk about feelings and experiences around sex that I don't want to talk about with anyone else.

Women and Sexuality

1. What does being sexual mean to you?

   To me, being sexual means: _____

   _____

   _____

   _____

   _____

   _____

   _____

2. How does being sexual relate to your self-esteem? _____

   _____

   _____

   _____

   _____

   _____

   _____

3. Has your sexuality changed over time as you have grown and changed as a woman? In what ways?

   _____

   _____

   _____

   _____

   _____

   _____

4. List ways in which you have felt sexually abused or harassed in your relationships.

   By your partner: _____

   _____

   _____

   _____

   _____

   _____

   _____

By a family member: _____

_____

_____

_____

_____

_____

_____

On the job: _____

_____

_____

_____

_____

_____

_____

In the media: _____

_____

_____

_____

_____

_____

_____

Other: _____

_____

_____

_____

_____

_____

_____

5. Do you feel powerful or powerless when being sexual? In what ways?

   *I feel:*_____

   _____

   _____

   _____

   _____

   _____

   _____

6. List ways to gain power and create self-esteem related to your sexuality.

   a. _____

   _____

   _____

   _____

   b. _____

   _____

   _____

   _____

   c. _____

   _____

   _____

   _____

7. Name two people with whom you can talk about women and sexuality.

   a. _____

   b. _____

"Twenty Years Too Late"

I've been married for over twenty years to a man who has abused me since early in our marriage. My career and children are the high points in my life. I shared with the group and the male guest presenter that I had received a dozen roses from my husband for Valentine's Day. A strange feeling came over me when I received the flowers: a mixture of anger, ambivalence, sadness, and resentment — but no excitement or joy, no happiness or love. My husband stood anxiously in front of me waiting for me to express my gratitude. I said to him, "The flowers are twenty years too late."

I explained to the group that he began crying and then pouted around the house for the rest of the evening. Then I began having doubts about what I'd said to him and I started to feel guilty. Maybe I was too hard on him and should have been more appreciative. Maybe he was really trying to change and I wasn't giving him the chance. I told the group that I really didn't want to give in to him and felt once again that I was being manipulated. At the time, I held my ground and stuck with my original thoughts and feelings.

I asked the male presenter, "Should I have been more receptive to his flowers? How do I know if he is really sincere about changing?" The male presenter gave me a quick response to the question when he said, "You don't." He said, "It may sound a bit too simple, but trust your gut." As the victim of his abuse, my gut instinct told me what I believed to be true — his flowers were twenty years too late. Both the group and male presenter affirmed that I need to trust my feelings and first take care of my emotional, physical, spiritual, and safety needs.

The group tonight helped me to confirm that I've suffered through twenty years of abuse; one night of flowers falls far short of what I'd hoped and dreamed of for my marriage. Even if he does change it may still be too late to make a difference in the relationship — the hurts are too deep and the risks are too great and I'm not sure if I want to be in this marriage any longer.

Questions about Men Who Batter

1. What are the main questions you have about men who batter?

   a. _____

   _____

   b. _____

   _____

   c. _____

   _____

2. What surprises you about some of the reasons given for why men batter?

   _____

   _____

   _____

   _____

   _____

3. What saddened you?

   _____

   _____

   _____

   _____

   _____

4. What gives you strength?

   _____

   _____

   _____

   _____

   _____

5. How will you use information you learn about why men batter to more clearly understand your situation?

   _____

   _____

   _____

   _____

   _____

"Shame Is about Me, Guilt Is about Behavior"

I have always felt so much guilt for putting my two sons through
two abusive relationships. Tonight in group our group discussion
was about shame and guilt. This was a topic I really needed to
hear. I learned that there is a difference between shame and guilt.
I learned that shame is about me as a person and that guilt is more
about behavior. I realized that I've felt a lot of shame since I was
very young. I told the group that I've felt a lot of shame for being in
not one, but two abusive relationships. Recently my oldest son told
me that he wants to live with his biological father. I feel like such a
failure as a mother. I've heard for years how I have failed as a mother,
so of course, I now say it to myself.

One woman in group said she felt it wasn't easy for me to talk
about the shame I've felt. A couple other women said they've felt
shameful feelings for being in abusive relationships too and hadn't
shared those feelings with anyone. We all agreed that we are *good*
moms and need to change our self-talk to something positive. I know
it won't be easy, yet I'm willing to try something I haven't tried
before. We ended group by each of us thinking of a positive statement
we could say daily to ourselves. I decided to tell myself, "As a mother,
I am doing a good job." I'm looking forward to going back to group
next week to report how good it felt to say positive statements to
myself.

Shame and Guilt

1. Look at these descriptions of shame and guilt:[1]

Shame	Guilt
I am a mistake.	I made a mistake.
I am a failure.	I failed to do something.
I am wrong.	My behavior is wrong.

   Which set of messages do you tend to give yourself? Why?

   _____

   _____

   _____

   _____

   _____

   _____

   _____

   _____

2. Do you feel shame or guilt about the abuse you've experienced?

   *I feel:*_____

   _____

   _____

   _____

   _____

   _____

   _____

3. What kinds of messages did you get as a child that caused you to feel ashamed or bad about yourself? (At home, at school, or from your peers).

   _____

   _____

   _____

   _____

   _____

   _____

   _____

[1] *Description of shame and guilt developed by Mary Jo Nissen, MD, LP, LICSW, St. Paul, Minnesota. Used by permission.*

4. Thinking about the cycle of shame,[2] can you fill in an example that is personal to you.

                    a. Negative behavior

    d. Tension and stress   b. Shame

              c. Cover-up behavior(s)

a. Negative behavior: (Example: Yelling at child.)

_____

_____

_____

_____

_____

b. Shame: (Example: Feeling like a bad parent.)

_____

_____

_____

_____

_____

c. Cover-up behavior(s): (Example: Drinking alcohol.)

_____

_____

_____

_____

_____

d. Tension and stress: (Example: Headache, hangover.)

_____

_____

_____

_____

_____

[2] *"Cycle of Shame" source unknown.*

5. How could you make changes in your shame cycle example for each of the following areas:

   a. Negative behavior: (Example: Count to ten before yelling.)

   _____

   _____

   _____

   _____

   _____

   b. Shame: (Example: Think of good things you have done as a parent.)

   _____

   _____

   _____

   _____

   _____

   c. Cover-up behavior(s): (Example: Call a friend - talk about your feelings.)

   _____

   _____

   _____

   _____

   _____

   d. Tension and stress: (Example: Rest with cold cloth on head.)

   _____

   _____

   _____

   _____

   _____

6. List three affirmations that you would like to give to yourself this week.

   a. _____

   _____

   b. _____

   _____

   c. _____

   _____

"Their Losses Were Somehow Mine"

Tonight's topic was one of the optional topics I hadn't voted for but am I ever glad it was voted in! When the group facilitator had us list losses we had experienced related to our abusive relationships, I was amazed at how many applied to my life. The topic really made me look at all the losses I've had in the past nine years. I told the group members about all the money I've spent in court trying to get the courts to protect me. I didn't receive any help I could count on so I finally had to move to another state without my children. Talk about a loss! Then I began to cry and feel some of the sad feelings I've kept in for so long. I told the group about having to change my identity so my ex-husband couldn't find me. I feel I have lost my self-esteem and my mental health all because of the abuse I have suffered for so many years that no one, it seemed, could do anything about.

I was amazed to hear the list of losses that other women in the group mentioned—I wasn't surprised at their losses, but astounded at all those I could identify with. Their losses were mine somehow. I guess many of us have lost and grieved over experiences common to being victims of abuse.

It felt good to get support from other group members who could also identify with experiencing grief and loss because of an abusive relationship. It helped to brainstorm as a group about ways to take care of ourselves because I haven't been doing that and I know I need to. It has really motivated me to practice one way to take care of myself this week. I like that the group facilitator is going to ask us next week what we did to take care of ourselves. This will hopefully force me to take some action to do something nice just for me.

Grief and Loss

1. List the losses in your life that have been significant to you. Describe how you feel about each.

   Loss: *I feel:*

   a. _____

   _____

   _____

   b. _____

   _____

   _____

   c. _____

   _____

   _____

   d. _____

   _____

   _____

2. Can you safely express these feelings? ___ yes ___ no

   If yes, who can you tell about these feelings? _____

   _____

   _____

3. List and explain the losses you have felt in your abusive relationship.

   a. _____

   _____

   _____

   _____

   b. _____

   _____

   _____

   _____

   c. _____

   _____

   _____

   _____

4. If you listed the loss of a partner, is it really the loss of that person or of a dream? Please explain.

_____

_____

_____

_____

_____

_____

5. How have your losses affected your self-esteem?

_____

_____

_____

_____

_____

_____

6. What happens if you do not allow yourself an opportunity to grieve your losses?

Physically: _____

_____

_____

_____

_____

Emotionally: _____

_____

_____

_____

_____

Spiritually: _____

_____

_____

_____

_____

7. List three ways you could take care of yourself when in grief.

   a. _____

   _____

   _____

   _____

   b. _____

   _____

   _____

   _____

   c. _____

   _____

   _____

   _____

"I Spent Three Days in Bed"

I just kept thinking over and over how stupid I was. Robert had left me and I knew no one else would ever want me. Why bother to go through the motions? It was just too hard. Even though Robert had abused me during the course of our seven-year marriage, I still felt totally wiped out when he finally left.

I spent three days in bed, only getting up to go to the bathroom. I was in a dark cloud, moving in slow motion. I had no energy and I wanted so badly to just evaporate. I thought constantly about killing myself but I didn't have the energy to do that, or anything else. I couldn't even take care of the kids. Andy made peanut butter sandwiches for me but I couldn't eat them. The cat even chewed on them but I didn't have the energy to shoo her away.

I wanted so badly to die. But I didn't want the kids to have to live with the stigma of having a mother who committed suicide. I didn't want them to grow up wondering why...I didn't want them to blame themselves for my problems. But I didn't think I could bear to see another day. I just wanted everything to be over.

Then a friend came over. She sat with me and told me about this women's group that her sister had gone to and about how it was a place for me to learn about what was happening to me. She practically picked up the phone and called for me. I've been to my third group meeting now, and I must say things are beginning to look up.
I am beginning to understand now that Robert had me so convinced of my worthlessness that, when he left, I thought no one would ever like or want me. Well, my group likes me—I really believe that, and I think that's a good first step out of this dark hole.

Depression

1. Describe periods in your life when you experienced depression.

   _____

   _____

   _____

   _____

   _____

2. What events or losses in your life may have contributed to being depressed?

   _____

   _____

   _____

   _____

   _____

3. How do you react to depression? What do you typically do?

   When I'm depressed I often: _____

   _____

   _____

   _____

   _____

   _____

4. What symptoms do you notice when you are depressed?
   (Example: Lack of energy).

   I notice: _____

   _____

   _____

   _____

   _____

5. Have you noticed any depression related to your abuse? Describe.

   _____

   _____

   _____

   _____

   _____

6. What helps you feel better when you're depressed? (Example: Walking, talking on the phone with a friend.)

*I feel better when I:*_____

_____

_____

_____

_____

7. Have you ever felt embarrassed or ashamed about your depression? Have you ever tried to hide it or keep it to yourself? Describe.

_____

_____

_____

_____

_____

8. What can you do to change that?

I can: _____

_____

_____

_____

_____

9. Are you aware of family members being depressed? Who are they and what do you know about their depression? (Think about grandparents, siblings, aunts, uncles, cousins, and other extended family members.)

_____

_____

_____

_____

_____

10. Name three people you can talk to about your depression.

a. _____

b. _____

c. _____

11. List five things you like to do alone or with someone else. Refer to this list when you feel depressed.

Things I like to do

Alone

1. _____
   _____
   _____

2. _____
   _____
   _____

3. _____
   _____
   _____

4. _____
   _____
   _____

5. _____
   _____

With someone else

1. _____
   _____
   _____

2. _____
   _____
   _____

3. _____
   _____
   _____

4. _____
   _____
   _____

5. _____
   _____

12. Depression is sometimes seen as a gift or as a positive in life. Can you write about something good or positive that may have come from being depressed? (Example: Time to think.)

_____
_____
_____
_____
_____
_____
_____
_____
_____
_____
_____
_____
_____
_____

"I've Put Everyone Else's Needs First"

I was really looking forward to group tonight. For the first time in a very long time, I feel good about myself. I was excited to share with my group members some things I've done to take care of me!

One of the things this group has done for me is to help me realize how much I've always done for others instead of myself. For most of my fifty-six years, I've taken care of others, put everyone else's needs first. I've raised my two children, supported two husbands, and now I'm raising my grandchild. I haven't felt happy or fulfilled in many years. When I think of all the time and energy I've put into this marriage and see no effort on Steve's part, I become very angry.

So tonight I shared with the group that I've started the process to find daycare and more help with my grandchild. I've ended marriage counseling until I see some concrete changes in Steve, I've redone my resume to find more stable employment, and I've begun to reconnect with some female friends. I can't believe how good I feel about myself and, best of all, I have so much more energy than I've had in the past.

Group members gave me lots of positive feedback. Loretta said she was impressed with all that I had accomplished in the past few weeks. Maureen said we need to tell ourselves it's okay to do things to take care of ourselves. The group leader said that it's important for all of us to think of ways to take care of ourselves and that sometimes writing a self-care plan can be helpful.

Self-Care

1. Describe your concept of self-care.

   *I think self-care means:*_____

   _____

   _____

   _____

   _____

2. Describe your energy level.

   *I am usually:*_____

   _____

   _____

   _____

   _____

3. What steps can you take to preserve some of that energy for your personal needs?

   I can: _____

   _____

   _____

   _____

   _____

   _____

   _____

   _____

   _____

   I can: _____

   _____

   _____

   _____

   _____

   _____

   _____

   _____

   _____

4. What are your self-care needs in the following areas?

Physical:_____

_____

_____

_____

_____

_____

_____

Emotional: _____

_____

_____

_____

_____

_____

_____

Intellectual: _____

_____

_____

_____

_____

_____

_____

5. What happens to you when you neglect your self-care?

_____

_____

_____

_____

_____

_____

_____

_____

6. Do you have any safety issues related to self-care?

_____

_____

_____

_____

_____

_____

_____

_____

_____

_____

7. How is your self-care sabotaged by a partner, children, family, or friends?

_____

_____

_____

_____

_____

_____

_____

_____

_____

_____

8. What would a one-year self-care plan include?

_____

_____

_____

_____

_____

_____

_____

_____

_____

_____

"Women Should Have an Equal Say"

When Ray and I first met, I thought I'd died and gone to heaven. He was so wonderful to my daughter and me back then that I could hardly believe how happy I was.

Then on Thanksgiving that first year, we were having my family over for dinner. I was so excited to be having my first real holiday dinner. About thirty minutes before people were due to arrive, Ray decided he wanted to have sex. He wouldn't take no for an answer and I finally gave in just to keep the peace. The rest of the day Ray pouted because I hadn't been responsive enough to suit him.

When I told the group that I didn't believe there was such a thing as a healthy relationship and that my friends all agree that men are babies unless they get their way, the group leader asked if everyone agreed with what I thought. Most did, but Joan in our group said that her sister has a wonderful husband who believes in equality between men and women.

The group leader said that she did not agree that all men are babies and that her experience was that there are mature men who treat women fairly. She thinks some men truly respect women versus using women for their own pleasure. She also said that women should have an equal say in deciding when they want to be sexual with their partners. Finally she said that the decision to have sex or not was just one of many decisions that in a healthy relationship are made by both partners.

This is confusing to me because my mother taught me that it was a woman's job to do whatever her man said, including having sex whenever he wanted it.

The group leader suggested that we all think about this, do some journaling on it, and talk to other women we respect and see what they think. Joan says she'll ask her sister about it and report back to the group. Right now, I can't imagine not feeling obligated to do whatever Ray wants. But who knows, maybe I can make some changes.

Healthy Relationships

1. Is your current relationship satisfying? ___ yes ___ no

   If no, why not? _____

   _____

   _____

   _____

   _____

   _____

   _____

   _____

   _____

   _____

   _____

   _____

   _____

   _____

2. In what ways are you neglecting yourself for the relationship?
   (Examples: Neglecting friendships, family ties, self-care needs.)

   _____

   _____

   _____

   _____

   _____

   _____

   _____

   _____

   _____

   _____

   _____

   _____

   _____

   _____

3. In what ways, if any, have you compromised your values for the relationship?

_____

_____

_____

_____

_____

_____

_____

_____

_____

_____

_____

_____

_____

_____

_____

_____

4. Can you flourish and grow as an individual in this relationship? If yes, why? If no, why not?

_____

_____

_____

_____

_____

_____

_____

_____

_____

_____

_____

_____

_____

_____

5. What things are you doing that you enjoy?

_____

_____

_____

_____

_____

_____

_____

_____

_____

_____

_____

_____

_____

6. What things would you like to add to your enjoyment list?

_____

_____

_____

_____

_____

_____

_____

_____

_____

_____

_____

_____

_____

"There Were Warning Signs"

I had been divorced from my abusive first husband for almost a decade when I finally met "Mr. Right." He looked perfect! He didn't raise his voice, didn't call me or anyone else names, and wouldn't dream of using physical force in any way. He was the exact opposite of my first husband and looked like a gem to me.

After two years of dating, we married. I had some subtle hints of the problems that might be coming, but I chose to ignore them. After all, it's hard to find a guy that works hard and doesn't raise his voice and I wanted to be cared for and married again. Within two months of marriage, George began to withdraw from me and the relationship. He didn't want to talk, became uncooperative socially, and would frequently hide behind a book or magazine with a drink in his hand. He also began complaining about my diminishing interest in our sex life and blamed me for not caretaking him properly. After trying to make the marriage work for several years, I finally decided to get help. As it turns out I ended up having to deal with abuse in both marriages as well as facing a second failed marriage. This was just not what I had in mind.

The group leader asked me what the early red flags were in my second marriage. I could remember that before we were married, George began monitoring my activity with friends and tried to tell me what time I had to be home. He thought I was too easy on my almost grown children and wanted them to have more rigid rules. He accused me of seeing old boyfriends and thought hang up calls were always meant for me. He didn't want to socialize with my family after awhile, and his sexual demands began to change. As I said, I ignored all this, thinking it would go away after we were married.

There were warning signs before the wedding ever took place. If I had confronted them early on, I probably wouldn't have married George. Someone else in the group mentioned that since I'd never addressed the abuse of my first marriage that that also may have contributed to my mistakes in choosing a new partner.

As I look back, I probably could have avoided this failed relationship by becoming more realistic about things and less idealistic about how "perfect" George was. I had set myself up for the knight on the white horse to save me. That doesn't work in real life.

Evaluating New Relationships

1. Explore how you think and feel when you are considering a new relationship.

   _____

   _____

   _____

   _____

   _____

   _____

   _____

2. List your expectations of a new relationship.

   _____

   _____

   _____

   _____

   _____

   _____

   _____

3. Name some of the ways in which you will evaluate a new partner for potential abusive behavior. (Example: Does he understand and support your schedule and obligations?)

   A new partner must: _____

   _____

   _____

   _____

   _____

   _____

4. What needs or wants will you communicate to a new partner?

   I need: _____

   _____

   I need: _____

   _____

   I need: _____

   _____

5. How soon in the relationship should you state these needs?

_____

_____

_____

_____

_____

_____

6. What are your fears about doing this?

_____

_____

_____

_____

_____

_____

7. How would you like to behave differently than you have in the past at the onset of a new relationship?

*I would:*_____

_____

_____

_____

_____

_____

8. Are you currently in a new relationship about which you have doubts, troubled feelings, or otherwise sense that something is just not quite right? What are your doubts?

_____

_____

_____

_____

_____

_____

9. If you are starting a new relationship, are you making decisions based on what your partner wants rather than what you want?

_____

_____

_____

_____

_____

_____

_____

10. How mature is your new partner? Does he act like a grown-up, like a teenager, or like a child?

_____

_____

_____

_____

_____

_____

_____

How does this affect you? _____

_____

_____

_____

_____

_____

_____

_____

_____

_____

_____

_____

_____

"My Life Feels More Hopeful"

Last night was the final session of my women's abuse group. I can't remember a time in my life when I felt so cared about by a group of women and was so sad to say good-bye. I can hardly believe that when next Wednesday comes, I won't have my group to go to. What a great thing in my life this group has been.

I'm thinking back right now to how I got to this group. I knew I needed help, but I had put off looking for help for so long that it just didn't seem to matter anymore. Then an incident brought the police to my door who gave me a phone number for victims of abuse.

I cannot possibly explain how I felt that first night of group. I was so scared and so sure that no one would understand me or my situation. But, for sixteen weeks now not only did most of the group members understand, but a couple had very similar situations.

The closing session made me feel so good about myself. We were given back the goals that we had set before the group started. I was so surprised to see how much progress I had made on some of my goals. I certainly discovered that I'm not alone and that the abuse is not my fault. I also have started to say "no" to people when they want me to jump and drop what I'm doing to help them. I learned a lot about the cycle of abuse and understand it better.

We had a great potluck meal together and reminisced about the past four months. Everyone agreed that four months sounded like an eternity to begin with, but passed quickly. After the dinner, every group member was asked to listen quietly while the other members told them about their strengths. When it was my turn, I started to feel nervous. What if no one could think of anything nice to say about me? As the group began telling me what they saw in me, I could hardly keep from crying. I've never had so many nice things said to me all at once. I came home with a list of 24 personal strengths.

This group was difficult, challenging, yet also one of the most important experiences in my life. My life feels more hopeful and I know that I'll be okay whether I have a partner or not. I know for the first time that I could be alone without falling apart. I have to thank the group for all their support and help. They have really made a difference in my life.

Closing Session

1. Your group has come to a close. How do you feel about it?

   _____

   _____

   _____

   _____

   _____

   _____

   _____

   _____

   _____

2. What is the most important thing you are taking away from the group for yourself?

   _____

   _____

   _____

   _____

   _____

   _____

   _____

   _____

   _____

3. Describe your plan for ongoing support. Be specific.

   My plan for ongoing support is: _____

   _____

   _____

   _____

   _____

   _____

   _____

   _____

4. What changes do you think you made during the course of group?

_____

_____

_____

_____

_____

_____

_____

5. How did it feel to have others recognize and state your strengths?

I felt: _____

_____

_____

_____

_____

_____

_____

_____

6. How do you feel about your progress on the goals you set for yourself?

_____

_____

_____

_____

_____

_____

_____

7. Which goals would you like to continue working on?

a. _____

b. _____

c. _____

8. What new goals would you like to set for yourself?

   Three-month goal: _____

   _____

   _____

   One-year goal:_____

   _____

   _____

   Five-year goal: _____

   _____

   _____

9. Was writing in this journal helpful for you? Do you plan to continue journaling?

   _____

   _____

10. What will you miss about the group members?

    I will miss: _____

    _____

    _____

    _____

    _____

    _____

11. Would you like to attend another group in the future? What kind of group?

    *I would like to attend:*_____

    _____

12. What is your best strength?

    *What I like best about myself is:*_____

    _____

    _____

    *because:*_____

    _____

    _____

    _____

    _____

Notes

Notes

Notes